• COLOUR YOUR WAY

BOTANICALS

by Edith Rewa

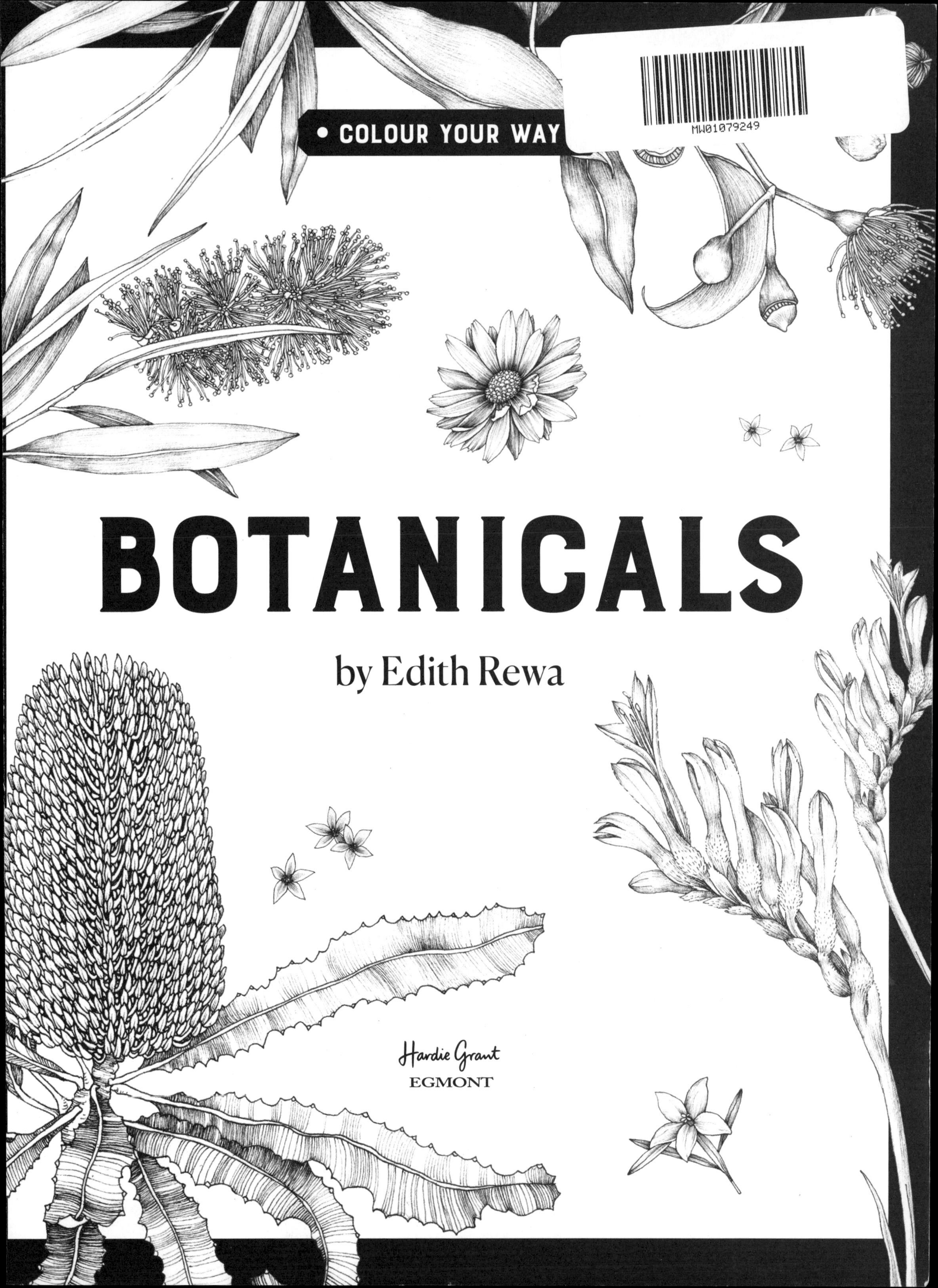

Hardie Grant
EGMONT

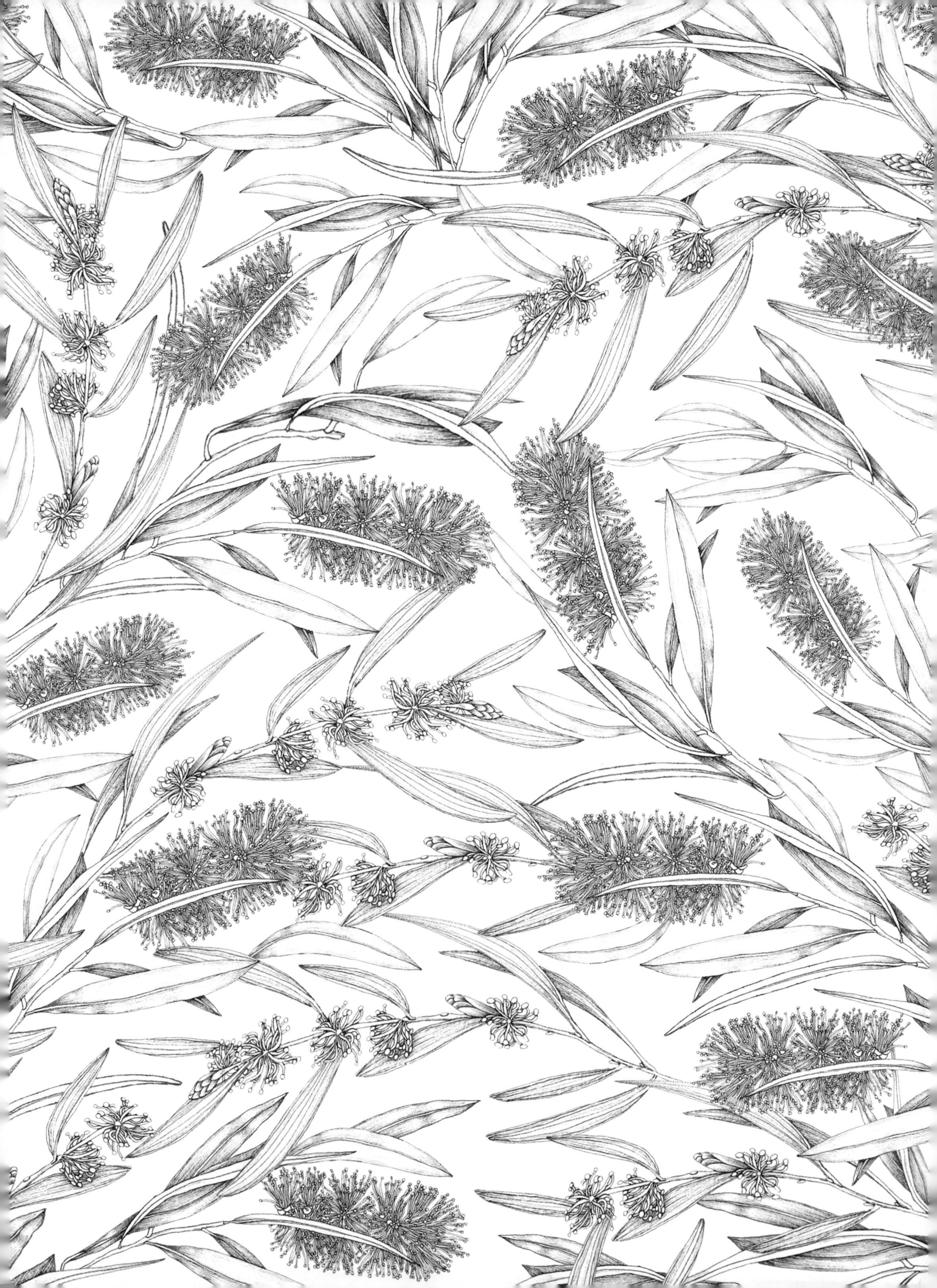

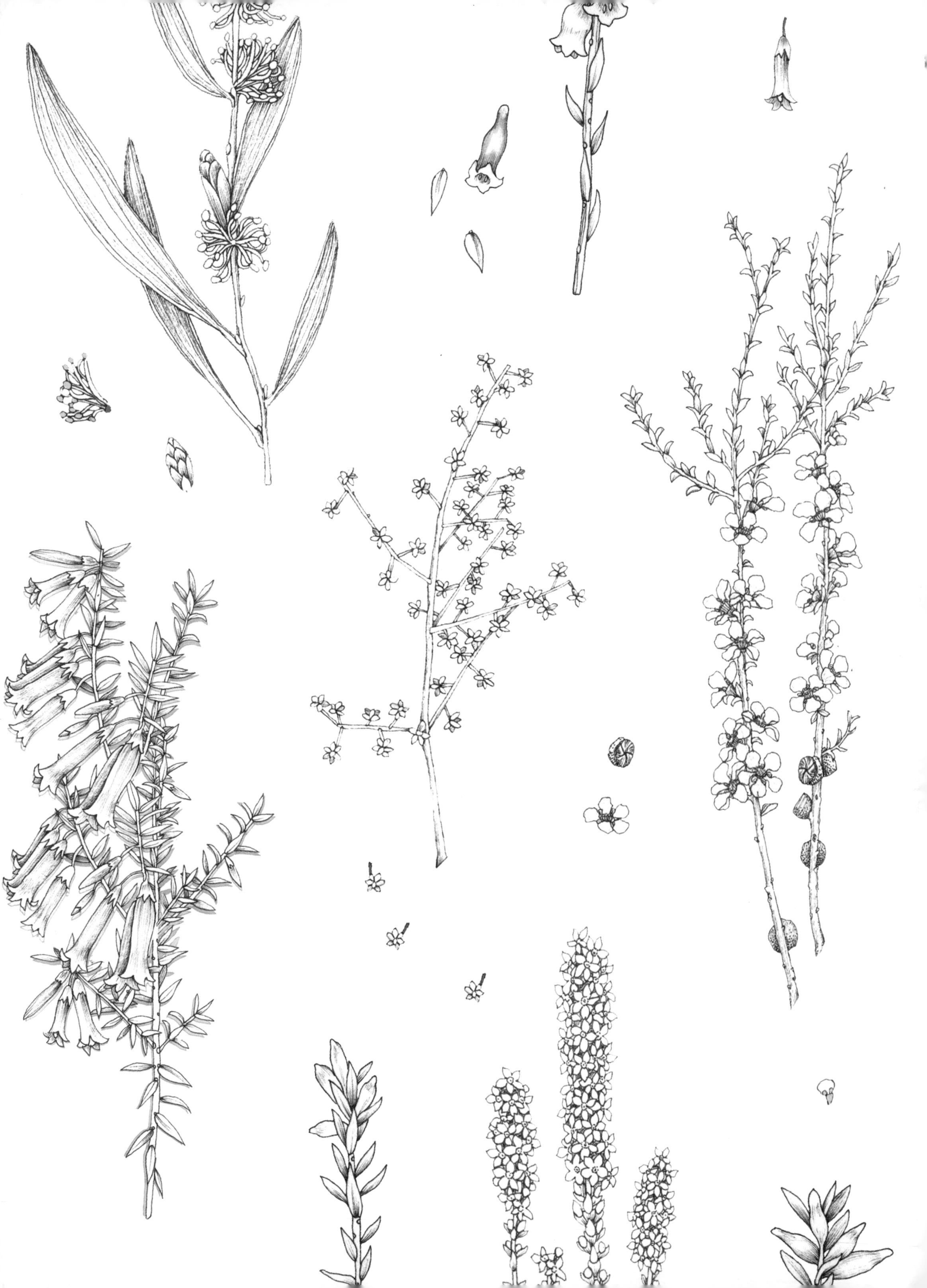

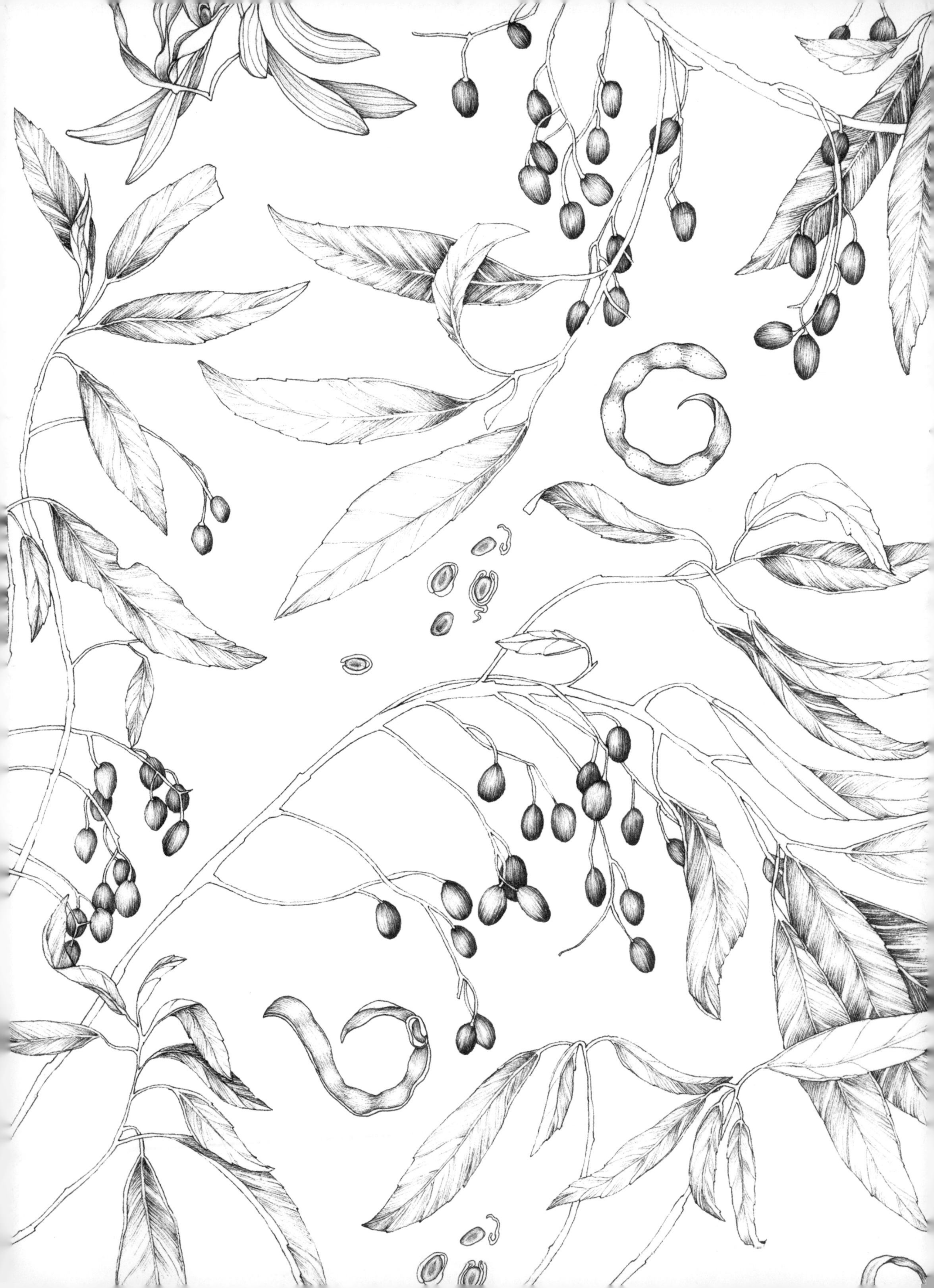

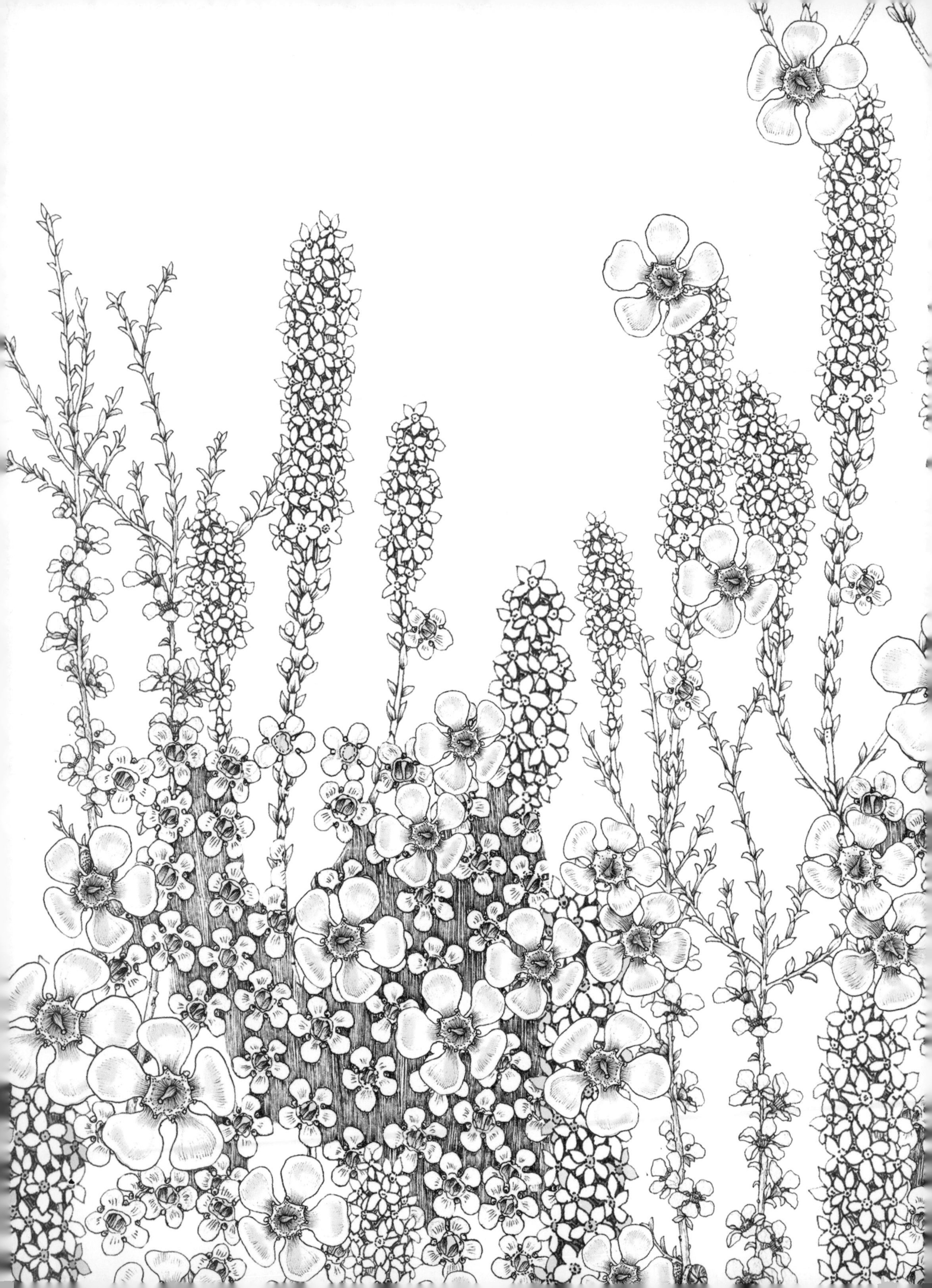

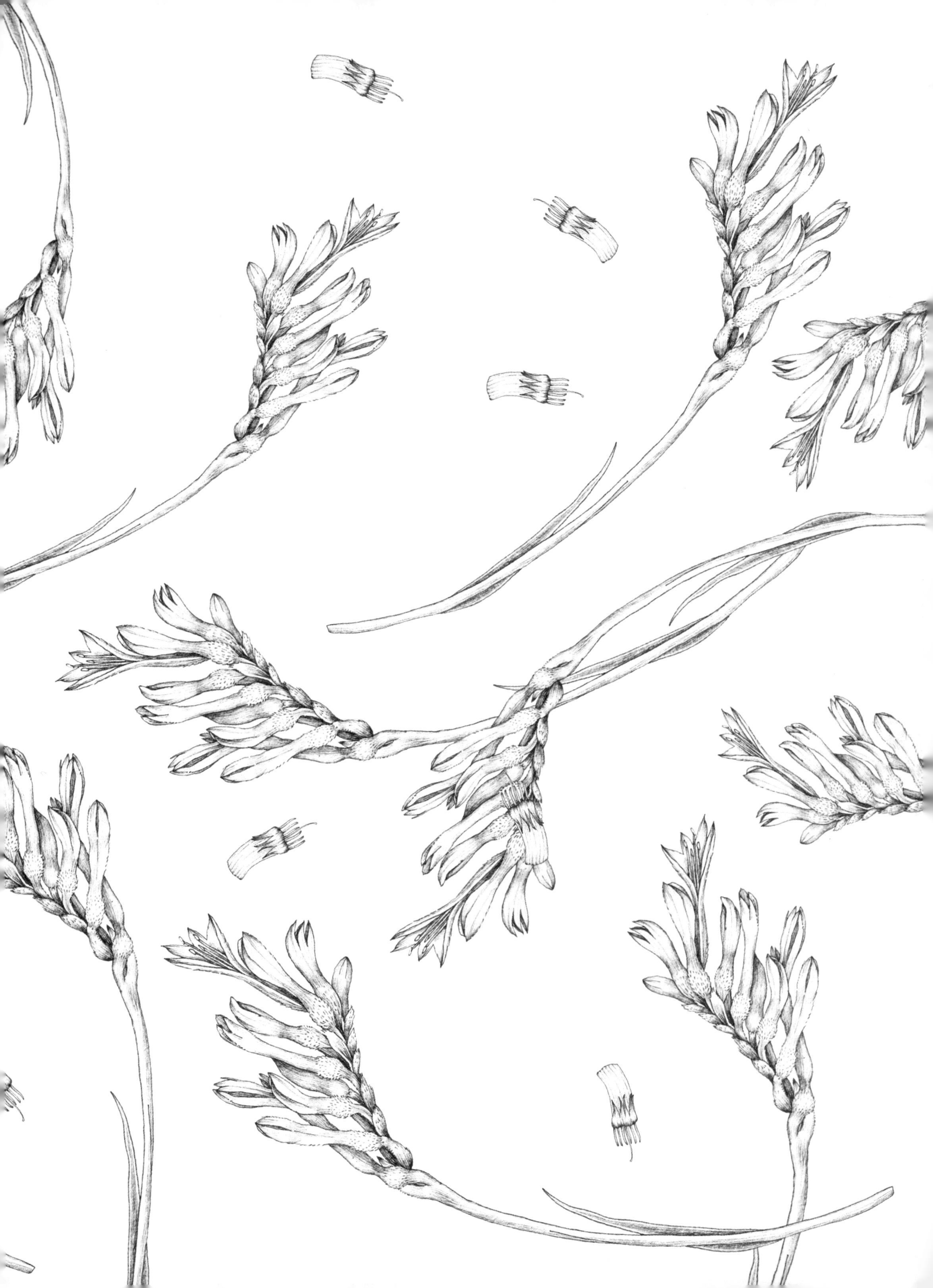